BUGS

By Caroline Lawton

SCHOLASTIC

NEW YORK · TORONTO · LONDON · AUCKLAND
SYDNEY · MEXICO CITY · NEW DELHI · HONG KONG

PHOTO CREDITS: front cover: javarman/Shutterstock; page 1: javarman/Shutterstock; page 3 caterpillar: Chas/Shutterstock; page 4 ant [top left]: Lletr/Shutterstock; page 4 ant [top right]: Mark Bowler/Photo Researchers; page 4 ant [bottom left]: Mark Bowler/Photo Researchers; page 4 aphids: Kletr/Shutterstock; page 5 bee [top left]: NickFree/iStockphoto; page 5 bee [top right]: Subbotina Anna; page 5 bee [center left]: Michel Gunther/Photolibrary; page 5 butterfly [center right]: Mitya/Shutterstock; page 5 butterfly [bottom left]: Kim Taylor/Minden Pictures; page 5 butterfly [bottom center]: Chungking/Shutterstock; page 5 butterfly [bottom right]: Elena Ray/Shutterstock; page 6 caterpillar [top left]: Cameramannz/Shutterstock; page 6 chrysalis: Bhathaway/Shutterstock; page 6 caterpillar [top right]: Voyagerix/iStockphoto; page 6 caterpillar [center]: Wild Wonders of Europe/Benvie/NPL; page 6 cricket [center right]: 2Happy/Shutterstock; page 6 cricket [bottom left]: PetrP/Shutterstock; page 7 clouds: Susan Mackenzie/Shutterstock; page 7 dragonfly [top]: Kim Taylor/NPL/Minden Pictures; page 7 dragonfly [bottom]: Catherine dée Auvil/iStockphoto; page 7 dung beetle [center right]: Antagain/iStockphoto; page 7 dung beetle [bottom left]: Melinda Fawver/Shutterstock; page 7 dung beetle [bottom right]: NHPA/Photoshot; pages 8–9 dirt: Cre8tive Images/Shutterstock; page 8 earwig [top]: Joseph Calev/Shutterstock; page 8 earwig [center]: Kim Taylor; page 8 emperor dragonfly [left]: Eric Isselee/Shutterstock; page 8 emperor dragonfly [center]: Alslutsky/Shutterstock; page 8 emperor dragonfly [right]: Eric Isselee/Shutterstock; page 9 firefly [top]: Norbert Wu/Science Faction/Corbis; page 9 firefly [inset]: Darwin Dale/Photo Researchers; page 9 small fly: Ioannis Pantziaras/Shutterstock; page 9 fly [center]: Tzara/iStockphoto; page 9 fly [bottom right]: Mark Bowler/Nature Picture Library; pages 10–11 grass: Edyta Pawlowska/Shutterstock; page 10 glowworm [top]: Henrik Larsson/Shutterstock; page 10 glowworm [inset]: Antinolo Jorge Sierra/Getty Images; page 10 glowworm [bottom]: Niall Benvie/Nature Picture Library; page 10 jumping grasshopper: Stephen Dalton/Nature Picture Library; page 10 grasshopper [right]: Arlindo71/iStockphoto; page 11 hornet [top center]: Kletr/Shutterstock; page 11 hornet [top right]: Stefan Sollfors/Science Faction/Corbis; page 11 hornet [center]: Mark Bowler/Nature Picture Library; page 11 small hornet: Triff/Shutterstock; page 11 hornworm [center]: Photodisc/Getty Images; page 11 hornworm [bottom]: Pablo H Caridad/Shutterstock; pages 12–13 leaves: Tanatat/Shutterstock; page 12 inchworm [top]: Arlindo71/iStockphoto; page 12 inchworm [center left]: Anna Diederich/Shutterstock; page 12 inchworm [center right]: Arlindo71/iStockphoto; page 12 io moth [left]: Norbert Wu/Minden Pictures; page 12 io moth [right]: David Kelly/Shutterstock; page 13 jewel beetle [top]: Pascal Goetgheluck/Photo Researchers; page 13 jewel beetle [center left]: Walter B. McKenzie/Getty Images; page 13 june bug [center right]: Brain Hagiwara/Getty Images; page 13 june bug [bottom left]: Sergey Chirkov/Shutterstock; page 13 june bug [bottom center]: Melinda Fawver/Shutterstock; page 14 tree: Michael J. Thompson/Shutterstock; page 14 katydid [top]: Yxm2008/Shutterstock; page 14 katydid [center]: Kim Taylor/NPL/Minden Pictures; page 14 katydid [bottom]: Yxm/Shutterstock; page 14 keeled treehopper [center]: Nicholas Richter/Mr. Nickon; page 14 keeled treehopper [bottom]: Nicholas Richter/Mr. Nickon; page 14 leaf: Dmitrjs Dmitrjevs/iStockphoto; page 15 ladybug [top right]: Arlindo71/iStockphoto; page 15 ladybugs [center]: Ale-ks/iStockphoto; page 15 ladybugs on grass: Antagain/iStockphoto; page 15 leafhopper [top]: Arlindo71/iStockphoto; page 15 leafhopper [center]: Arlindo71/iStockphoto; page 15 leafhopper [bottom]: Arlindo71/iStockphoto; page 16 mantis [top]: Pushlama/iStockphoto; page 16 mantis [bottom]: Andersboman/iStockphoto; page 16 moth [top]: Choja/iStockphoto; page 16 moth [center]: Rqsinboxru/iStockphoto; page 16 moth [bottom]: Choja/iStockphoto; page 17 narcissus bulb fly [top]: Anne Sorbes/Getty Images; page 17 fly on flower: Christian Musat/Shutterstock; page 18 orange-tip butterfly: Renphoto/iStockphoto; page 18 Oregon swallowtail [center]: Jens Stolt/Shutterstock; page 18 Oregon swallowtail [bottom]: Carlos E. Santa Maria; page 18 sunflower: White_Bcgrd/Shutterstock; page 19 painted lady butterfly [top]: Cathy Keifer/Shutterstock; page 19 painted lady butterfly [bottom]: Alslutsky/Shutterstock; page 20 queen butterfly [top left]: Ogphoto/iStockphoto; page 20 butterfly [top right]: Alslutsky/Shutterstock; page 20 question mark butterfly [bottom left]: John A Anderson; page 20 question mark butterfly [bottom right]: Badjoby/Wikipedia; page 21 red ants on grass: Antagain/iStockphoto; page 21 red ant [top right]: Alex Wild/Visuals Unlimited; page 21 tiny ants: Dreamframer/Shutterstock; page 21 rhinoceros beetle [left]: Defun/iStockphoto; page 21 rhinoceros beetle [right]: Sad444/iStockphoto; page 21 orchid: Shutterstock; page 22 scorpion [top left]: BSIP/Photo Researchers; page 22 scorpion [top right]: Arkady/Shutterstock; page 22 spider [center left]: David Good/Shutterstock; page 22 spider [bottom left]: D&K Kucharscy/Shutterstock; page 22 spider on web: Feng Yu/Shutterstock; page 23 tarantula [top]: Matthew Cole/Shutterstock; page 23 tarantula [center]: Kim Taylor/Nature Picture Library; page 23 tarantula [bottom]: Kim Taylor/NPL/Minden Pictures; page 23 tick [left]: Dennis, David M./Animals Animals; page 23 tick [right]: Kim Taylor/Nature Picture Library; page 24 umbrella wasps: Antagain/iStockphoto; page 24 wasp on nest: Zhuda/Shutterstock; page 25 velvet mites: Nigel Cattlin/Visuals Unlimited; page 25 viceroy butterfly [center]: Cathy Keifer/iStockphoto; page 25 viceroy butterfly [bottom]: Cybernesco/iStockphoto; pages 26–27 water: Vilnis Lauzums/Shutterstock; page 26 wasp [top left]: Kim Taylor/NPL/Minden Pictures; page 26 wasp [top right]: Alle/Shutterstock; page 26 wasp [center left]: Eric Isselee/Shutterstock; page 26 wasp [center right]: Pan Xunbin/Shutterstock; page 26 wasp [bottom left]: Pan Xunbin/Shutterstock; page 26 water strider: Knorre/Shutterstock; page 26 brown bug [center bottom]: Francois Gilson/Photolibrary; page 27 Xerces blue butterfly: The Field Museum, #Z94225_19c; page 28 yellow crane fly [top left]: Francois Gilson/Photolibrary; page 28 yellow crane fly [top right]: Biosphoto/Hette Stéphane/Peter Arnold; page 28 yellow jacket wasp [center]: Melinda Fawver/Shutterstock; page 28 wasp [bottom left]: Antagain/iStockphoto; page 28 yellow jacket wasp [bottom center]: Brendan Howard/Shutterstock; page 28 yellow jacket wasp [bottom right]: Brooke Whatnall/Shutterstock; page 29 zebra spider [top center]: D&K Kucharscy/Shutterstock; page 29 spider [top right]: Bogdanhoria/iStockphoto; page 29 zebra spider [center]: D&K Kucharscy/Shutterstock; page 29 zebra swallowtail butterfly: Dorling Kindersley/Getty Images; back cover: Igor Gorelchenkov/Shutterstock

ISBN 978-0-545-27330-5

10 9 8 7 6 5 4 3 2 1 11 12 13 14 15

Printed in the U.S.A. 40
First edition, January 2011

Design by Kay Petronio
Photo research by Alan Gottlieb

Whether they are flying, crawling, or hopping, bugs are special creatures. Let's take a close look at bugs, from

A to Z.

A

Ant

Ants live together in groups called **colonies**. Some ants live for a few weeks. Other ants live for many years.

Aphid

Aphids are tiny insects. Each aphid is only the size of a pinhead, but together they can damage many plants.

Bee

Bees have five eyes, but none of them can see the color red.

Butterfly

Butterflies taste food with their feet. A butterfly sucks its food through a tube that unrolls from its head.

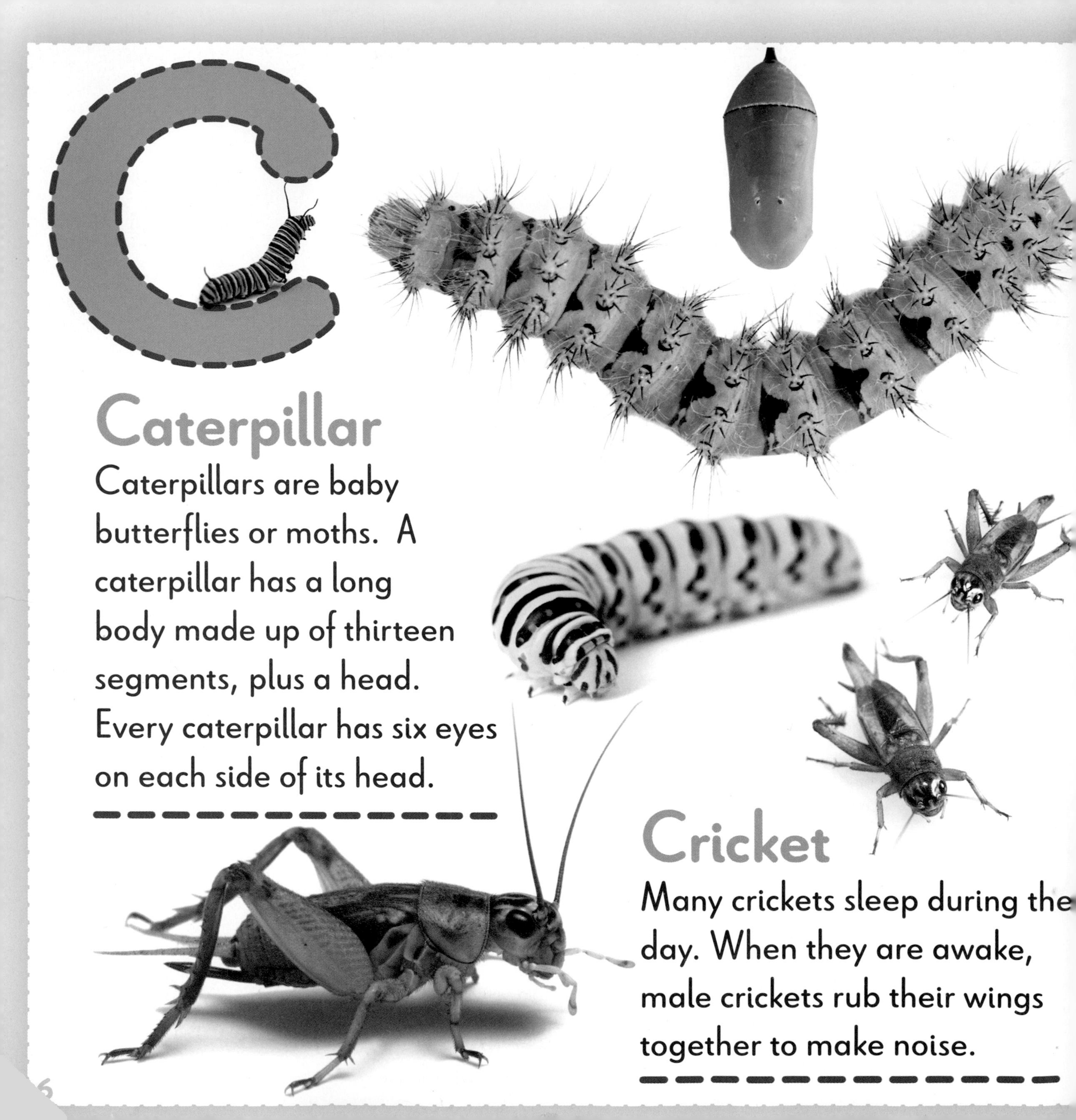

Caterpillar

Caterpillars are baby butterflies or moths. A caterpillar has a long body made up of thirteen segments, plus a head. Every caterpillar has six eyes on each side of its head.

Cricket

Many crickets sleep during the day. When they are awake, male crickets rub their wings together to make noise.

Dragonfly

Dragonflies have six legs, but they cannot walk. Instead, they use their wings to fly.

Dung beetle

Dung beetles eat poop. Before they eat it, they roll it into small balls.

E

Earwig

Earwigs like to hide. Their long, flat bodies help them fit into small places.

Emperor dragonfly

Emperor dragonflies live near rivers and lakes. Males have blue bellies. Females have bright green bellies.

Firefly

The light from a firefly can be yellow, green, or red. Large groups of fireflies can work together so they all blink at the same time.

F

Fly

Flies cannot eat solid food. They spit on their food to make it soft. Then they drink it.

Glowworm

Only glowworm **larvae** and adult female glowworms glow. They glow a blue-green or yellow-green color.

Grasshopper

Grasshoppers are known for jumping. They can jump more than six feet at a time.

Hornet

Hornets chew wood and plants to make a paste. Then they use the paste to make their nests.

Hornworm

Hornworms are some of the largest caterpillars. They can grow to be four inches long.

I

Inchworm

Inchworms are not worms at all! They are actually caterpillars.

Io moth

Io moths' wings have a pattern that can scare aw animals that will eat then called **predators**.

Jewel beetle

There are many kinds of jewel beetles. They come in very bright colors, like green, blue, orange, and even purple.

June bug

June bugs hide during the day. At night, they eat plants and flowers.

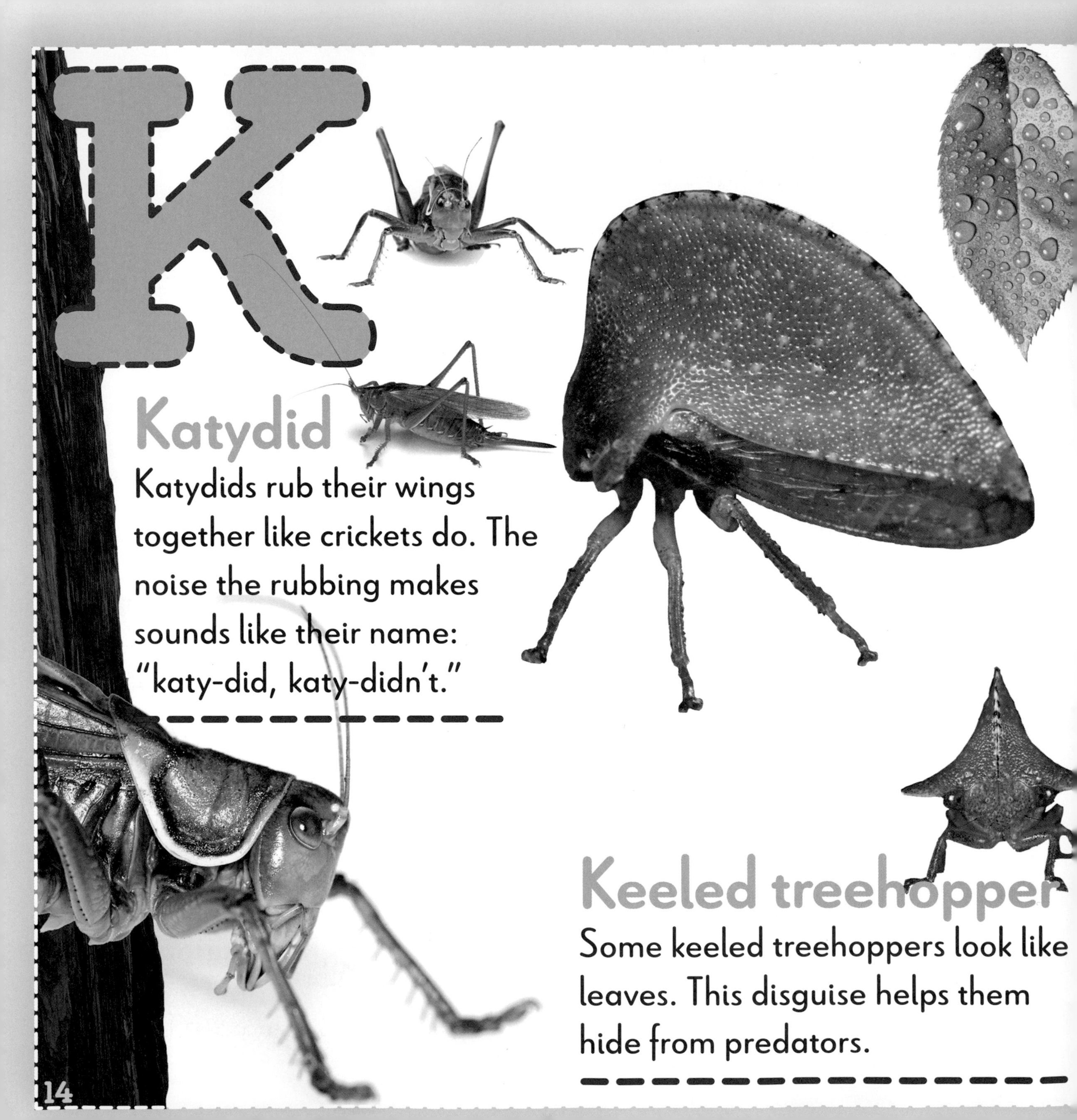

K

Katydid

Katydids rub their wings together like crickets do. The noise the rubbing makes sounds like their name: "katy-did, katy-didn't."

Keeled treehopper

Some keeled treehoppers look like leaves. This disguise helps them hide from predators.

Ladybug

Not all ladybugs have the same number of spots. Some have no spots. Others have as many as twenty-four.

Leafhopper

Leafhoppers have special mouths shaped like straws. All leafhoppers eat tree **sap**.

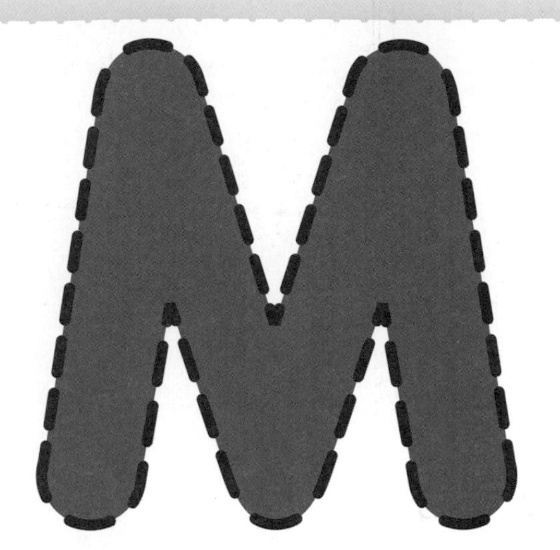

M

Mantis

Mantises use their two front legs to catch their food. Mantises can eat insects, frogs, and even other mantises.

Moth

At night, moths can sometimes be spotted flying around lights. The atlas moth is the largest moth.

Narcissus bulb fly

Narcissus bulb flies look like bees, but they do not sting.

N

Orange-tip butterfly

Only male orange-tip butterflies have orange on the tips of their wings. Female orange-tip butterflies have white wings.

Oregon swallowtail

Oregon swallowtail butterflies drink **nectar**, the liquid inside flowers. This butterfly is the state insect of Oregon.

Painted lady butterfly

Painted lady butterflies are known for their colorful wings. They **migrate** from North Africa to Europe every summer.

Queen butterfly

Female queen butterflies lay eggs on milkweed plants. When the eggs hatch, the baby caterpillars eat the plants' leaves.

Question mark butterfly

Question mark butterflies get their name from the shape of their wings. The front set of wings forms the shape of a question mark.

Red imported fire ant

Red imported fire ants can sting. Their sting is painful and their poison can be deadly.

R

Rhinoceros beetle

Rhinoceros beetles are some of the strongest insects on the planet. They are also some of the largest.

S

Scorpion

Scorpions have poisonous stingers. The poison inside their stingers is called **venom**.

Spider

All spiders have eight legs, but not all of them make webs. A spider's web is used to catch their **prey**.

Tarantula

Tarantulas are big, hairy spiders. Unlike many other spiders, they do not make webs. Instead, tarantulas live in trees or underground.

Tick

Most ticks live in the woods or in fields. They can live for up to three years.

U

Umbrella wasp

Umbrella wasps get their name from the shape of their nests. Their nests look like upside-down umbrellas.

Velvet mite

Velvet mites are known for their bright red color. Their bodies are covered in tiny hairs.

Viceroy butterfly

Viceroy butterflies are often mistaken for monarch butterflies. They have orange and black wings.

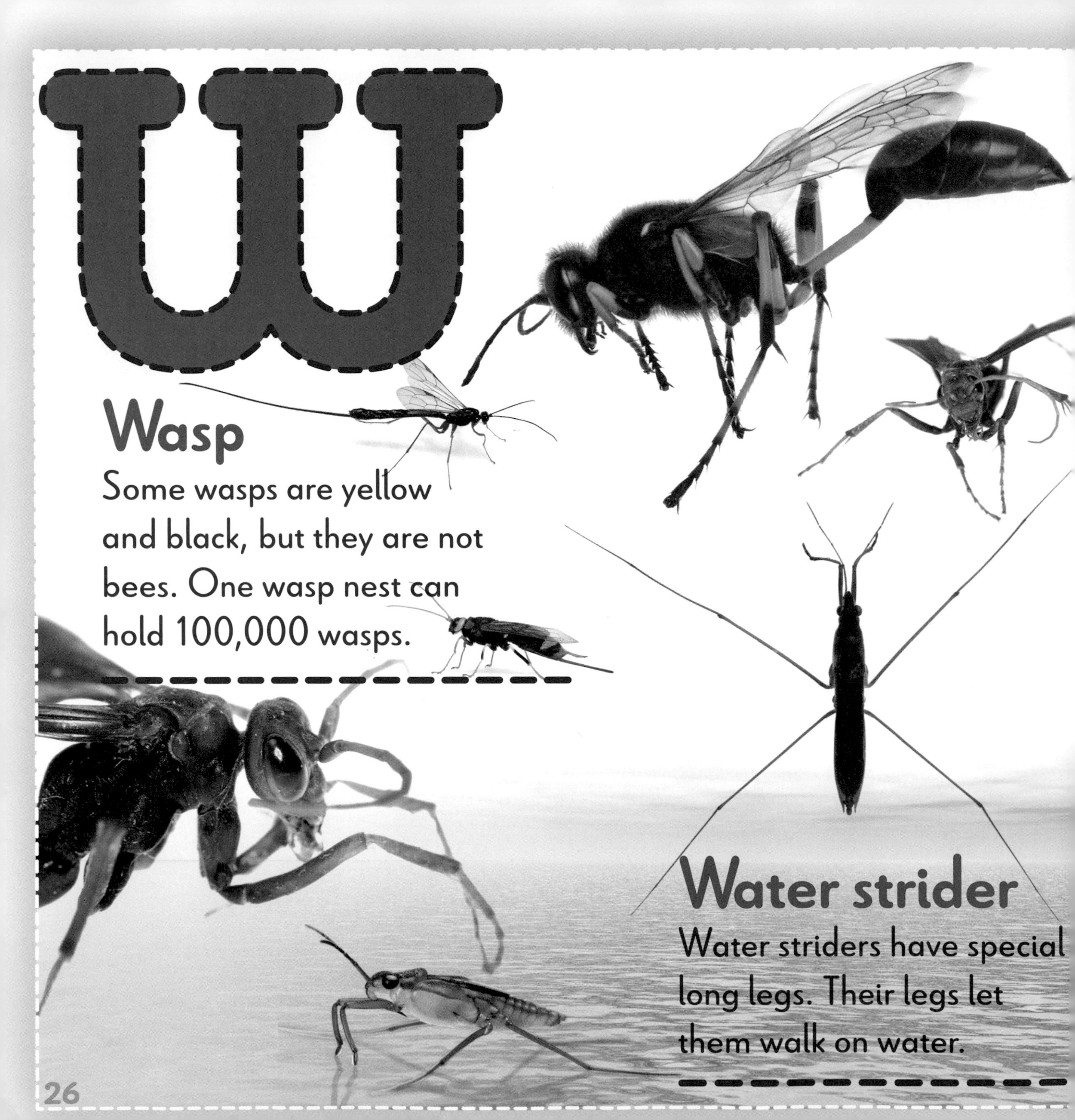

W

Wasp

Some wasps are yellow and black, but they are not bees. One wasp nest can hold 100,000 wasps.

Water strider

Water striders have special long legs. Their legs let them walk on water.

Xerces blue butterfly

Xerces blue butterflies have been **extinct** since the 1940s. They were known for their bright blue wings.

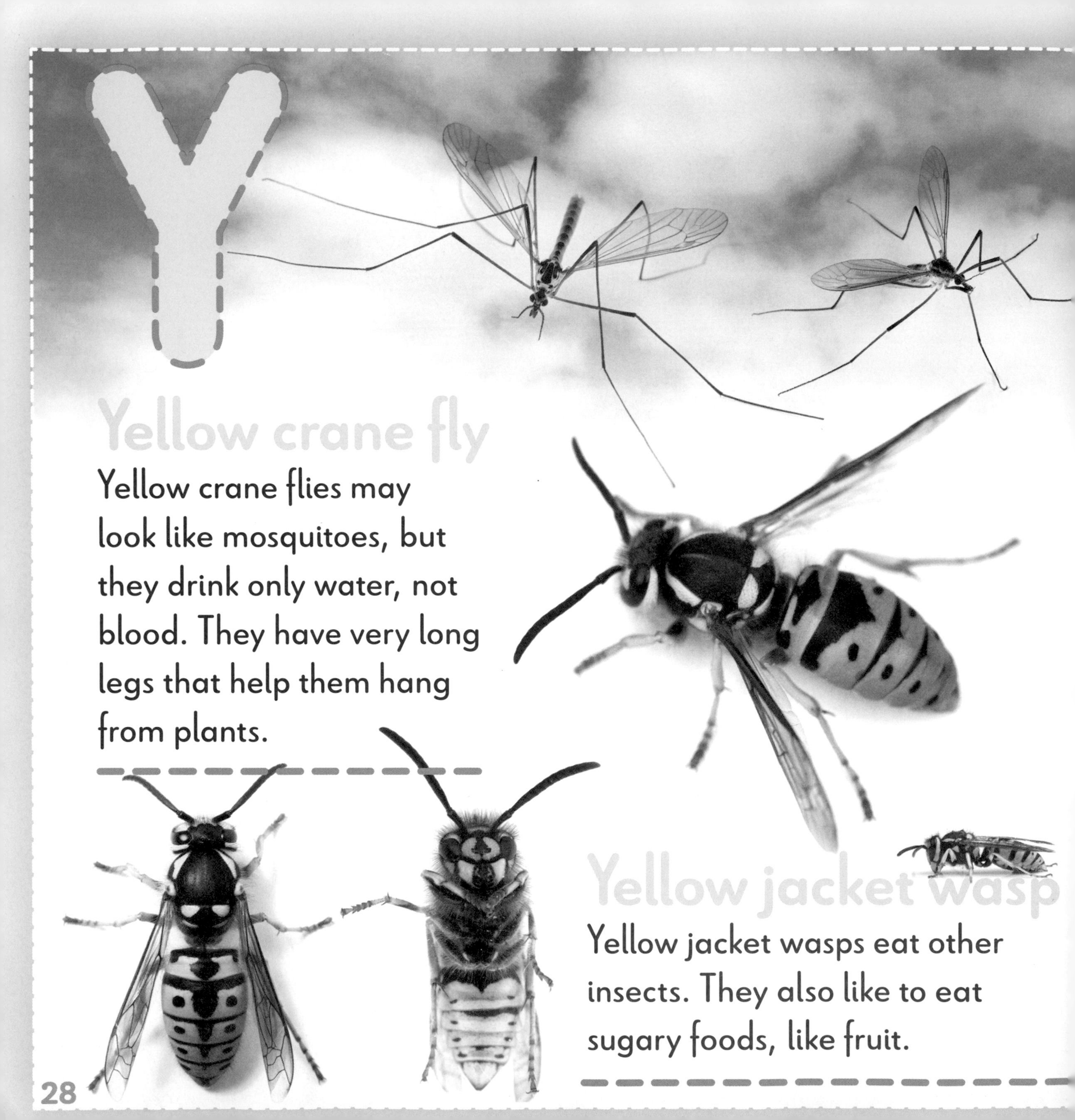

Y

Yellow crane fly

Yellow crane flies may look like mosquitoes, but they drink only water, not blood. They have very long legs that help them hang from plants.

Yellow jacket wasp

Yellow jacket wasps eat other insects. They also like to eat sugary foods, like fruit.

Zebra spider

Zebra spiders are a kind of jumping spider. They jump on their food. Zebra spiders do not build webs like many other spiders do.

Zebra swallowtail butterfly

Zebra swallowtail butterflies have black-striped wings. They also have long tails like zebras!

Bugs come in all shapes and sizes, from A to Z. There are even more fun bug facts just waiting to be found!

Glossary

Colony—a group of insects living together

Extinct—does not exist anymore

Larva—the form an insect takes between birth and adulthood

Migrate—to travel from one place to another

Nectar—the sweet liquid found inside flowers

Predator—an animal that hunts and eats other animals to survive

Prey—an animal that is hunted by another animal for food

Sap—the liquid found inside a plant

Venom—the poison made by animals

Index